The
Moneran
Kingdom

The Moneran Kingdom

REBECCA STEFOFF

Marshall Cavendish
Benchmark
New York

Marshall Cavendish Benchmark
99 White Plains Road
Tarrytown, New York 10591
www.marshallcavendish.us

Editor: Karen Ang
Publisher: Michelle Bisson
Art Director: Anahid Hamparian
Series design by Patrice Sheridan

Library of Congress Cataloging-in-Publication Data

Stefoff, Rebecca, date
The Moneran kingdom / by Rebecca Stefoff.
p. cm. — (Family trees)
Includes bibliographical references and index.
Summary: "Explores the habitats, life cycles, and other characteristics of organisms in the Moneran kingdom"—Provided by publisher.
ISBN 978-0-7614-3076-6
1. Microbiology—Juvenile literature. 2. Prokaryotes—Juvenile literature. I. Title.
QR57.S74 2009
579—dc22
2008023210

Front cover: *Staphylococcus* bacteria found on the skin
Title page: *Clostridium* bacteria
Back cover: *Streptococci* bacteria

Photo research by Candlepants, Incorporated
Front cover: David Scharf / Getty Images
The photographs in this book are used by permission and through the courtesy of:
Photo Researchers Inc.: Dr. Kari Lounatmaa, 3, 48, 55; CNRI, 9, 49; Alfred Pasieka, 11; Steve Gschmeissner, 18; Dr Tim Evans, 32; Eye of Science, 34, 61; Biophoto Associates, 52; Dr. Jeremy Burgess, 53; Karsten Schneider, 57; Volker Steger, 65; B. Murton/Southampton Oceanography Centre, 68; Scimat, 70. Alamy Images: PHOTO-TAKE Inc., 6, 38, 43, 29, 75(lower), 79, 85; Medical-on-Line, 8, 81, 83(left); Peter Arnold, Inc., 30, 50, 84(left); Greenshoots Communications, 60; blickwinkel, 69; Dave Bevan, 74; Libby Welch, 75(top); The Print Collector, 77; Mary Evans Picture Library, 78; Holt Studios International Ltd, 83(right). Shutterstock: 7, 19, 37, 71. Getty Images: Dr. Fred Hossler/Visuals Unlimited, 13; Dr. Gopal Murti/Visuals Unlimited, 36; Gary Buss, 40; Michael Rosenfeld, 42; M.I. Walker/Dorling Kindersley, 44; Dr. Terrence Beveridge/Visuals Unlimited, 46. Corbis: Frans Lanting, 14, 72; Chris Boydell/Australian Picture Library, 67: Chris O'Rear, 84(right). The Image Works: Ann Ronan Picture Library/HIP/, 20; SSPL, 25, 21, 23; Science Museum/SSPL/, 26. Visuals Unlimited: Ralph Slepecky, 45; Ralph Robinson, 59; Ken Lucas, 73. US Department of the Interior, National Park Service: Bob Lindstrom, 63. SuperStock: Image Source, back cover.

Printed in Malaysia
1   3   5   6   4   2

CONTENTS

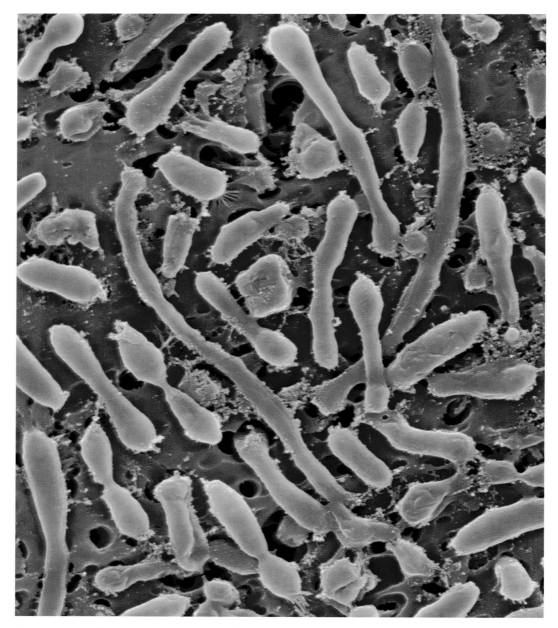

These single-celled creatures, photographed through an electron microscope, are extremophiles—monerans that live in extreme conditions. Scientists discovered them in water more than twice as salty as normal sea water.

Classifying Life

-Without a microscope you cannot see the great majority of life on Earth. You cannot see the monerans, living things that are so small that they are invisible to the unaided eye. If you added together all the monerans in the world, then added together all the visible plants, animals, and fungi, right down to the last mosquito and flower seed, the microscopic monerans would outweigh the macroscopic, or visible, life by at least ten times, according to biologist Colin Tudge, author of *The Variety of Life*.

People usually call monerans by a different name: bacteria. These microorganisms consist of just a single cell, but they are hardy, able to live almost anywhere—deep in the soil, on the ocean floor, even inside human stomachs. Monerans are not only the most numerous and widespread life forms in the world, they are also the oldest. Scientists think that monerans were the first living things to develop on Earth, and that all other organisms evolved from them.

We live in a bacterial world, surrounded by an enormous variety of invisible creatures. The influence of these organisms on human beings is both negative and positive. One of their biggest effects is on our health. Bacteria make us sick. Depending on the bacterium involved, the sicknesses

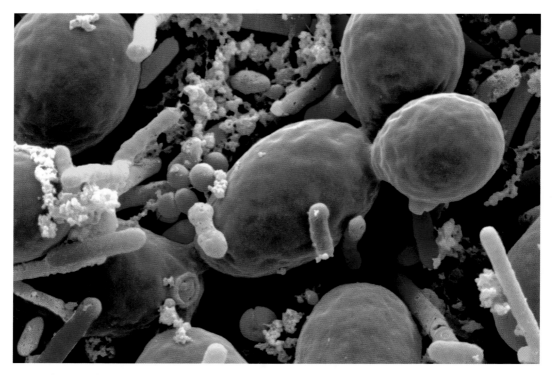

Many food-making processes require bacteria and other microorganisms. In this close-up of sauerkraut, or fermented cabbage, the blue rods are lactic acid bacilli, bacteria that produce natural antibiotics. The greenish globes are yeast, a type of fungus.

they cause range from a mild case of food poisoning to deadly diseases such as malaria, tuberculosis, or anthrax.

Yet bacteria are essential to some ancient industries, such as the making of cheese and yogurt, and to some new ones, such as developing strains of bacteria that can eat plastic waste and environmental toxins. Bacteria also decompose dead plant and animal matter, enrich the soil, produce oxygen, and make it possible for plants to grow. Monerans, in short, make the Earth habitable and hospitable to life. To understand how they are related to other microorganisms, and how they fit into the natural world, it helps to know something about how scientists classify living things.

THE INVENTION OF TAXONOMY

Science gives us tools for making sense of the natural world. One of the most powerful tools is classification, which means organizing things in a pattern according to their differences and similarities. Since ancient times, scientists who study living things have been developing a classification system for living things. This system is called taxonomy. Scientists use taxonomy to group together organisms that share features, setting them apart from other organisms with different features.

Taxonomy is hierarchical, which means that it is arranged in levels. The highest levels are categories that include many kinds of organisms. These large categories are divided into smaller categories, which in turn are divided into still smaller ones. The most basic category is the species, a single kind of organism.

The idea behind taxonomy is simple, but the world of living things is complex and full of surprises. Taxonomy is not a fixed pattern. It keeps changing to reflect new knowledge or ideas. Over time, scientists have developed rules for adjusting the pattern even when they disagree on the details.

One of the first taxonomists was the ancient Greek philosopher Aristotle (384-322 BCE), who investigated many branches of science, including biology. Aristotle arranged living things on a sort of ladder, or scale. At the bottom were those he considered lowest, or least developed, such

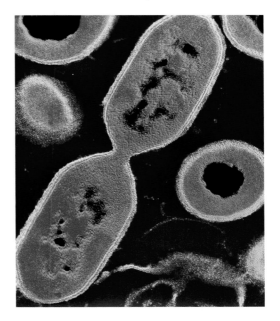

Monerans such as these *Listeria* bacteria were unknown to the first taxonomists. Early systems of classifying life dealt only with organisms visible to the unaided eye.

as worms. Above them were things he considered higher, or more developed, such as fish, then birds, then mammals. Microorganisms such as the monerans, however, were completely unknown in Aristotle's time.

For centuries after Aristotle, taxonomy made little progress. People who studied nature tended to group organisms together by features that were easy to see, such as separating trees from grasses or birds from fish. However, they did not try to develop a system for classifying all life. Then, between 1682 and 1705, an English naturalist named John Ray published a plan of the living world that was designed to have a place for every species of plant and animal. Ray's system was hierarchical, with several levels of larger and smaller categories. It was the foundation of modern taxonomy.

Swedish naturalist Carolus Linnaeus (1707–1778) built on that foundation to create the modern system of taxonomy. Linnaeus was chiefly interested in plants, but his system of classification included all living things. Its highest level of classification was the kingdom. To Linnaeus, everything belonged to either the plant kingdom or the animal kingdom. (He placed microorganisms, which had been discovered in the late seventeenth century, in the animal kingdom.) Each kingdom was divided into a number of smaller categories called classes. Each class was divided into orders. Each order was divided into genera. Each genus—the singular form of genera—contained one or more species.

Linnaeus also developed another of Ray's ideas, which was a method for naming species. Before Linnaeus published his important work *System of Nature* in 1735, scientists had no recognized system for referring to plants and animals. Organisms were generally known by their common names, but many of them had different names in various countries. Two naturalists might call the same plant or animal by two different names—or use the same name for two different organisms.

To end the confusion, so that scholars everywhere could communicate clearly about plants and animals, Linnaeus started the practice of giving each plant or animal a two-part scientific name made up of its genus and species. These names were in Latin, the scientific language of Linnaeus's

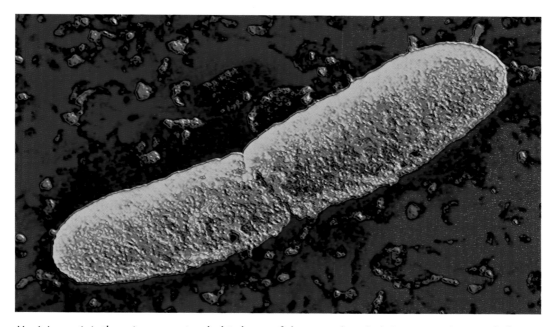

Yersinia pestis is the microorganism behind one of the most dreaded diseases in history: bubonic plague. After a terrible outbreak in the fourteenth century, Europeans called this sickness the Black Death.

day. For example, the bacterium that causes bubonic plague is *Yersinia pestis,* or *Y. pestis* after the first time the full name is used. The genus *Yersinia* contains a number of bacteria, some of which cause diseases in human beings. The bacterium responsible for bubonic plague is set apart from the other bacteria in the genus by the second part of its name, *pestis,* which is the Latin word for plague or disease.

Linnaeus named hundreds of species. Other scientists quickly adopted his highly flexible system to name many more. The Linnaean system appeared at a time when European naturalists were exploring the world and finding thousands of new plants and animals. This flood of discoveries was overwhelming at times, but Linnaean taxonomy helped scientists identify and organize their finds.

Classifying a Bacterium

Bacteriologists divide bacteria and archaea into subgroups that may be called either phyla or divisions. Often, however, bacteriologists ignore the middle taxonomic levels—class, order, and family—because these have not been established for many species,

Long clusters of cyanobacteria, or blue-green algae, form a rippling mat in a stream.

and be- cause bacterial classification tends to change frequently. The important levels of classification are genus and species. Some species are further broken down into subspecies, or into variant forms called strains. The Taxonomic Outline of Bacteria and Archaea, frequently updated with new data from genetic studies of monerans, lists the

Even at the highest level of classification, scientists take different approaches to taxonomy. A few of them still divide all life into two kingdoms, plants and animals. At the other extreme are scientists who divide life into thirteen or more kingdoms. Some taxonomists use categories called superkingdoms or domains. Most scientists, though, use classification systems with five to seven kingdoms: plants, animals, fungi, and several kingdoms of microscopic organisms such as bacteria, amoebas, and algae.

The classification of living things is always changing, as scientists learn more about the connections among organisms. The monerans are no exception. In the 1970s, researchers discovered that some monerans are not bacteria at all. Instead they are a completely different kind of life, called the species that have been identified in each phylum (by order, class, and family, if these are known).

The bacterium *Prochlorococcus marinus* is found in the world's oceans in vast numbers. Here is its scientific classification.

Kingdom	Monerans (bacteria and archaea)
Domain	Bacteria
Phylum or Division	Cyanobacteria (bacteria that manufacture energy from sunlight through photo synthesis; also called blue-green algae)
Family	Cyanobacteria 1.1 (subgroup of cyanobacteria that share a particular arrangement of genetic material)
Genus	*Prochlorococcus* (subgroup of very small cyanobacteria 1.1 that are found in oceans and contain a distinctive form of chlorphyll)
Species	*marinus* (one of several species of *Prochlorococcus*)

archaea. Although bacteria and archaea share some important basic features, the genetic differences between them are so profound that taxonomists now consider the bacteria and the archaea to be two of just three great branches on the tree of life. All other living things are on the third branch.

Today, research on bacteria and archaea is one of the liveliest frontiers in biology. Experts think that these microorganisms have much to teach us about the origin and development of life on our planet. And because some bacteria and archaea thrive in extreme cold or heat, or in chemicals that would kill most other forms of Earth life, the monerans may hold clues about the kinds of life that could exist on other worlds as well.

THE FIVE

Many scientists divide Earth's

ANIMALIA

polar bear

FUNGI

mushroom

MONERA

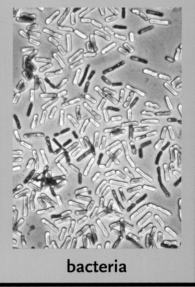

bacteria

KINGDOMS

life-forms into five kingdoms.

PLANTAE

pitcher plants

PROTOCTISTA

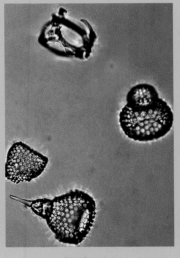

radiolarians

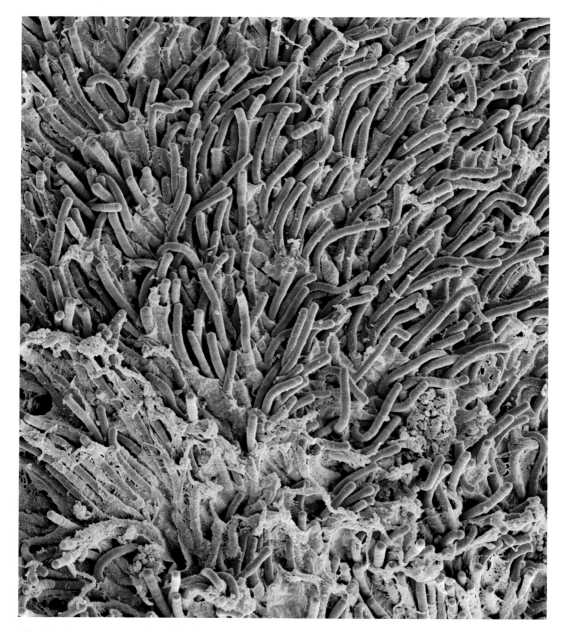

The first bacteria ever described were seen in dental plaque like this. Plaque consists of bacteria (pink rods) embedded in a substance formed from human saliva and bacterial waste. Acids in the waste weaken tooth enamel.

Into the Invisible World

On September 17, 1683, a Dutch merchant and scientist named Antoni van Leeuwenhoek discovered tiny creatures living inside his mouth. Leeuwenhoek used a microscope to examine "a little white matter" that he had scraped from between his teeth. A modern dentist would call this white matter plaque (and would advise regular dental care to remove it). In a letter to the Royal Society, a British scientific organization, Leeuwenhoek told what he saw when he looked at the white matter through his microscope:

> . . . many very little living animalcules, very prettily a-moving. The biggest sort. . . had a very strong and swift motion, and shot through the water (or spittle) like a pike does through the water. The second sort. . . ofttimes spun round like a top. . . and these were far more in number.

"Animalcules," or little animals, was Leeuwenhoek's name for the moving organisms he saw through his microscope. Those creatures living in plaque are now known to be bacteria, some of the smallest living things, and Leeuwenhoek made the first known observations of them.

Leeuwenhoek and other early pioneers of the microscope found that the world is filled with invisible life. Their discoveries launched the science

Antoni van Leeuwenhoek opened the eyes of the world to the existence of the tiny, invisible organisms he called "little animals."

of microbiology, the study of microorganisms. Today microbiology is in the midst of revolutionary advances brought about by genetic science and technology. The ability to decode the genetic material inside cells is creating new views of how the microscopic monerans fit into the tree of life.

PIONEERS OF MICROSCOPY

By the mid-seventeenth century, European scientists were experimenting with the design and construction of microscopes. With their instruments they began carrying out systematic examinations of the natural world. Microscopy, the art and science of using microscopes, was developing. Two of its most important pioneers were Robert Hooke in England and Leeuwenhoek in the Netherlands.

Hooke was a man of many interests: an astronomer, chemist, architect, and inventor. He built a number of microscopes, all of which had at least two lenses. The best of them magnified objects about thirty times. Through these instruments Hooke studied minute features of the natural world: bees' stings, a silkworm's thread, the skin of a plum. Hooke marveled at the unexpected beauty of small things. When he looked at a flea through his microscope, he thought its outer shell looked like a suit of polished black armor.

In 1665 Hooke published a book called *Micrographia,* which contained drawings and descriptions of the wonders he had observed through his microscopes. It

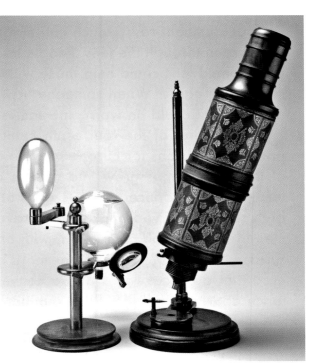

Robert Hooke used the device on the left to light the specimens he viewed through the microscope. It consists of an oil lamp, a globe filled with liquid to intensify the light, and a lens to project the light onto the specimen.

also told how he had built the instruments. *Micrographia* introduced readers to the strange new realm of the microworld. One reader was Antoni van Leewenhoek, who took up microscopy around 1668.

Leeuwenhoek had two big advantages as a microscopist. First, his eyesight was unusually keen at very short ranges. Second, he developed great skill as a microscope maker. Leeuwenhoek built hundreds of microscopes, mostly in a style he invented, each with a single small but very strong lens. These instruments were more like magnifying glasses than microscopes, but with them Leeuwenhoek could enlarge things by up to two hundred times and see details down to about one micrometer, or 1/25,000 of an inch. With these powerful devices Leeuwenhoek discovered living things so small that no one had ever seen them before.

He first saw these "animalcules," as he called them, in 1674, when he looked at a drop of lake water through one of his microscopes. To his astonishment, the droplet that had appeared clear to his unaided eyes was filled with tiny objects: green blobs and wriggling swimmers. The blobs were algae, a form of microscopic plant life. The swimmers were tiny creatures known today as protozoa.

Leeuwenhoek shared his discoveries in letters to Hooke and the Royal Society in England. In the years that followed he looked for animalcules in all kinds of substances: cheese, soil, water from many sources, even human and animal feces. His descriptions of the minute creatures he found were so precise and accurate that biologists today can easily recognize most species. Among Leeuwenhoek's discoveries were a number of "very little animalcules," such as the ones he saw in the plaque from between his teeth. He had discovered the smallest living organisms. Later they would be named bacteria.

Hooke, Leeuwenhoek, and other early microscopists revealed that the world is inhabited by multitudes of tiny living things, invisible to ordinary sight. These minute organisms exist even on, and inside, human beings. Throughout the eighteenth century, as instrument makers developed more powerful microscopes, curious people continued to investigate the

In 1828 an artist used the public's growing familiarity with microorganisms to criticize London's drinking water. The cartoon's original caption reads: "Monster Soup, commonly called Thames Water, being a correct representation of that precious stuff doled out to us!"

microscopic world. By the nineteenth century, scientists knew of the existence of a large variety of single-celled microorganisms. As biologists continued to study these microscopically small life forms—which they called both microorganisms and microbes—the new science of microbiology emerged.

INSIDE THE CELL

An early milestone of microbiology was the discovery of plant and animal cells. As early as 1665 Robert Hooke had described looking through his microscope at a piece of cork. He saw that the cork was made up of many tiny compartments. He called them cells because they reminded him of the cells, or small rooms, that monks inhabited in a monastery. The term came

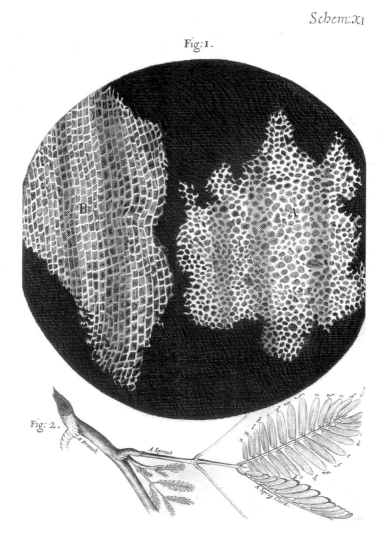

Robert Hooke illustrated the microscopic structure of cork in his 1665 book, calling the small compartments in the cork cells. Scientists now use his term for the structural units of all living things.

into use to describe the small structures that are the building blocks of plants and animals.

By the mid-nineteenth century microscopists had established that all plant and animal tissues are made up of many cells. Individual cells absorb nutrients and produce energy. They multiply by dividing, or splitting in two. Scientists had also determined that every cell has an outer coating called a cell wall and internal structures called organelles.

Inside a plant or animal cell, many of the internal structures are enclosed within membranes of their own. The largest of these membrane-enclosed structures, and the first to be seen by microscopists, was called the nucleus. When cells divide, so do their nuclei (which, scientists now know, contain most of the cells' genetic material).

All cells in macroscopic organisms have nuclei. Among the single-celled microscopic organisms, however, some species have nuclei and some do not. In microorganisms that do not have nuclei, the organelles simply float around inside the cell wall. These species of microorganisms are called non-nucleated.

In the twentieth century the two kinds of cells acquired new scientific names. Nucleated cells became eukaryotes, and non-nucleated cells became prokaryotes. (The names come from the Greek word *caryon*, which means kernel or center.) By that time, the smallest known microorganisms had another name as well. These prokaryotic or non-nucleated microbes, mostly shaped like rods or staffs, were called bacteria, from the Greek word *bacterion*, "small staff."

FIVE KINGDOMS

Nineteenth-century biologists recognized that some microorganisms have cell nuclei and others do not, but they did not think that the difference between eukaryotes and prokaryotes was very significant. One leading biologist of the late nineteenth and early twentieth centuries, Ernst Haeckl

Measuring Microorganisms

To measure bacteria and other tiny objects that are visible only through microscopes, scientists have had to define special units of measurement. These units are fractions of the meter, which is equal to 39.4 inches, or almost 3.3 feet.

Millimeter (mm)	One thousandth of a meter (0.039 inches, or a bit more than 1/25th of an inch)
Micrometer or micron (µm)	One-millionth of a meter (a thousand times smaller than a millimeter)
Nanometer (nm)	One-billionth of a meter (a thousand times smaller than a micrometer)
Angstrom (Å)	One ten-billionth of a meter (ten times smaller than a nanometer)

The cells of living things are too small to be seen with the unaided eye. Cells in plant and animal tissues, as well as eukaryotic microorganisms (single-celled organisms that have nuclei), are typically 10 to 100 µm long or across. Some are smaller. Human red blood cells, for example, measure about 5 µm across.

Prokaryotic microorganisms (bacteria and archaea) are smaller than most eukaryotic microorganisms. Some of the smallest bacteria are members of the genus *Chlamydia,* which measure about 0.2 µm. Even smaller monerans, called nanobacteria, have been reported, but bacteriologists do not yet know much about them. Among the largest bacteria are the spirochetes, which reach lengths of up to 250 µm. An exceptionally large bacterium called *Epulopiscium fishelsoni,* which lives inside surgeon fish in the oceans, can be as long as 600 µm—more than half a millimeter. Most bacteria, however, never get larger than 1 to 10 µm in length or diameter. Viruses, which are not living organisms, are smaller than bacteria. They range from 0.1 to 0.05 µm in size. Small molecules of matter are less than a nanometer across, while individual atoms are measured in angstroms.

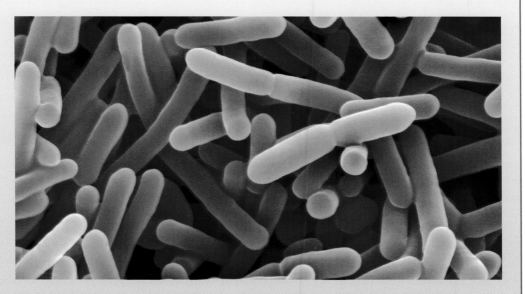

Bifidobacteria belong to a genus of gut flora, or microbes that live in healthy human intestines. They are a typical size for bacteria, averaging about 5 micrometers (about 1/5,000th of an inch) in length or diameter.

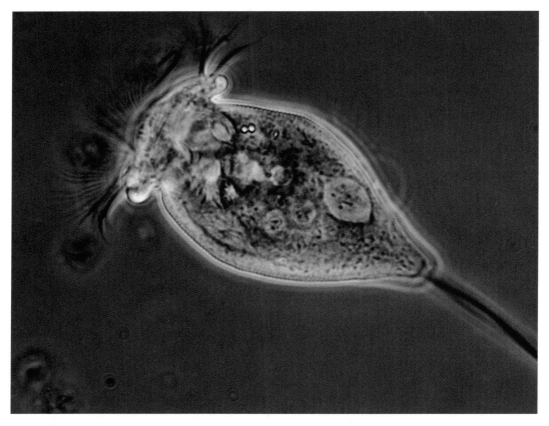

Vorticella, a single-celled water-dwelling protozoan, is a eukaryote, which means that it has a cell nucleus. Some of the major structures inside the cell are grouped together within a membrane, rather than floating freely as in monerans.

of Germany, grouped the two kinds of microorganisms together when he revised Linnaean taxonomy. Linnaeus had identified only two kingdoms, plants and animals, but Haeckl created a third kingdom, the protists. This kingdom contained all single-celled microorganisms, with and without nuclei. Haeckl did, however, give the two types of microbes their own names. He called the non-nucleated ones monerans and the nucleated ones protozoans.

Haeckl's three-kingdom taxonomy broke down in the mid-twentieth century, for two reasons. Biologists recognized that the fungi were fundamentally different from both plants and animals and deserved a kingdom of their own. They also divided single-celled microbes into two kingdoms: one for non-nucleated prokaryotes and one for nucleated eukaryotes. The result was a system of five kingdoms: monerans (bacteria), protoctists (microorganisms with nuclei), fungi, plants, and animals. Of the five kingdoms, one was prokaryotic and four were eukaryotic.

THREE DOMAINS

The five-kingdom taxonomy remains in use today, but alongside it is a new view of life based on the work of Carl Woese, a biologist at the University of Illinois. In the 1970s Woese wanted to study the evolutionary history of all life, hoping to discover how all the different categories were related to one another. This is an enormous task, but Woese approached it through something small: a single gene.

Genes are life's software—the instructions that tell cells what proteins to manufacture to create an organism. A typical gene consists of a thousand or so units of chemical information called nucleotides. Over time, random changes called mutations alter the order of nucleotides in genes. Organisms pass these changes to their offspring, which inherit their parents' genetic material.

To find out how long ago two organisms evolved away from a shared ancestor, scientists look at the same gene in both organisms, then count the differences in the sequence of nucleotides. If there are few differences, the organisms have not been evolving separately for long—maybe just a few million years. If there are a lot of differences, the lines leading to the two organisms separated much further back in time.

For his study, Woese focused on a gene found in all living things. It is called 16S rRNA, or ribosomal RNA. Woese started mapping the sequence

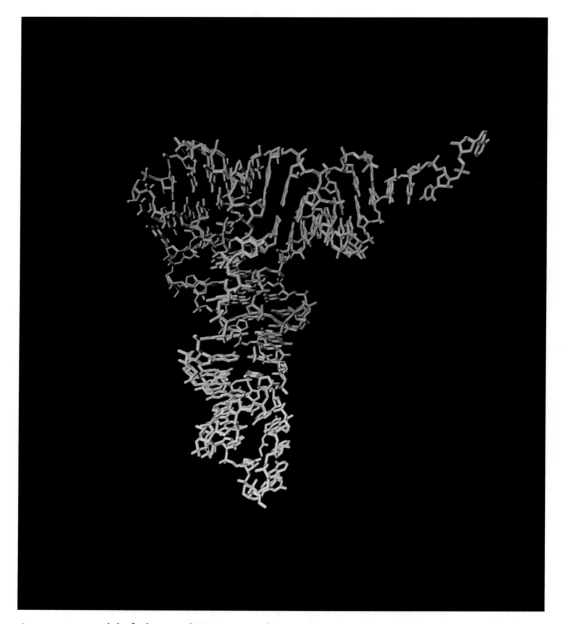

A computer model of ribosomal RNA uses colors to show that it is made up of many different strands. Ribosomal RNA, the molecule that turns acids into proteins within cells, was the key to discovering a new tree of life.

of nucleotides for the 16S rRNA gene in a variety of organisms. By comparing the sequences, he could create a tree of life that would show how all organisms are related, and when the various branches separated from each other.

As Woese analyzed the ribosomal RNA from organism after organism, he saw that certain sequences of nucleotides on the 16S rRNA gene reflected the fundamental division of life into two basic categories. One category

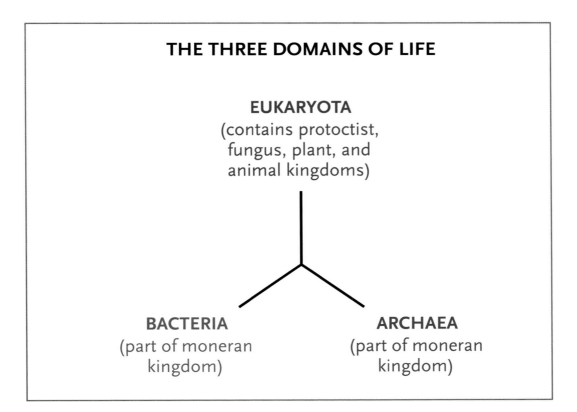

THE THREE DOMAINS OF LIFE

EUKARYOTA
(contains protoctist, fungus, plant, and animal kingdoms)

BACTERIA
(part of moneran kingdom)

ARCHAEA
(part of moneran kingdom)

The discovery of the archaea led to a view of life that recognizes three large categories called domains. Two domains, Bacteria and Archaea, form the kingdom of monerans or prokaryotes (microorganisms without cell nuclei). The third domain, Eukaryota, contains all other living things—all of which are eukaryotes, or organisms with cell nuclei. Within this domain are the kingdoms of animals, plants, fungi, and the microorganisms called protoctists.

was the prokaryotes—the monerans or bacteria, which are microbes without cell nuclei. The other category was the eukaryotes—every form of life *except* the bacteria. Each category had a distinctive nucleotide sequence. This pattern was pretty much what Woese had expected. Then one day he encountered a microbe that did not fit the pattern.

That microbe was a methanogen, a microorganism that produces methane gas. It was also a thermophile, or heat-lover. It lived in the waters of natural hot springs. Woese could see that the microbe lacked a nucleus, which made it a prokaryote. But its 16S rRNA gene did not have the

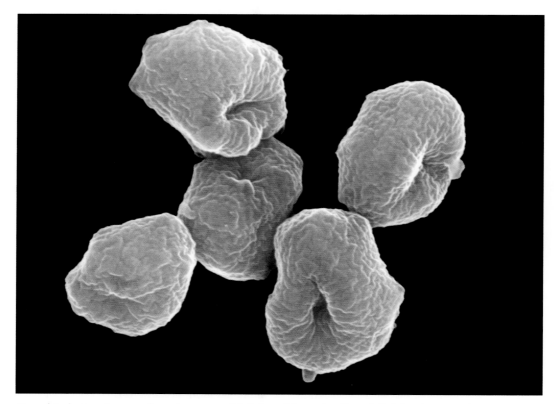

Found in hot springs and environments high in acids and sulfur, *Sulfolobus* is an archaeon, a member of a little-known group of prokaryotes that was discovered in the 1970s.

sequence of nucleotides that Woese had found in every other prokaryote. It did not have the eukaryote sequence, either. Woese realized that the mysterious microbe belonged to a completely different, unknown branch on the tree of life.

Since that time, researchers have examined the ribosomal RNA of many microbes. They have found a deep division within the prokaryotes, or monerans. Many of these one-celled organisms would once have been classified as bacteria, but their 16S rRNA gene, like that of Woese's original mystery microbe, is different from that of bacteria.

In the late 1970s, Woese suggested dividing all life into three categories that he called domains. The domain Eukaryota contains all of the eukaryotes: animals, plants, fungi, and microorganisms that have cell nuclei. The domain Bacteria, not surprisingly, contains the bacteria. For the prokaryotes that are different from bacteria, Woese chose the name archaea. He placed them in their own domain, Archaea. Scientists now have two overlapping ways of looking at life on Earth. Living things belong to three domains, and they also belong to five (or more) kingdoms.

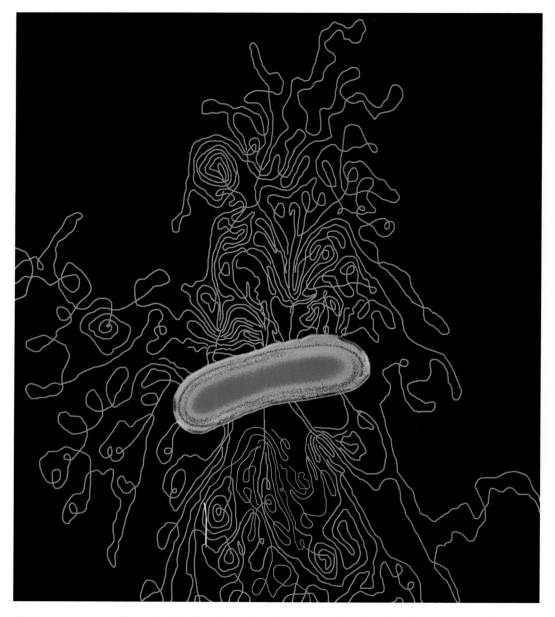

DNA streams out of a cell of *Escherichia coli,* a bacterium often found in the intestines of mammals, including humans. The discovery that monerans can exchange DNA was one of many surprises in modern bacteriology.

Bacteria and Archaea

Bacteria and archaea are a lot alike. Both are monerans or prokaryotes, which are microbes that do not have cell nuclei. They live and reproduce in similar ways. The general term "bacteria" sometimes includes both kinds of microbes, because much of what scientists have learned about bacteria since the nineteenth century applies to the archaea, too.

Bacteriology, as the study of bacteria is called, is part of the larger science of microbiology, which is concerned with all microorganisms. A lot of bacteriological research over the years has focused on practical matters, such as the role of these microbes in industry and in disease. At the same time, scientists have gained insight into the structure and life cycle of prokaryotes, and about their ecological roles—the ways they interact with other organisms and with their environments.

TYPES OF BACTERIA

All bacteria are single cells, but those cells come in a wide variety of shapes. A spherical or ball-shaped bacterium is called a coccus, while a long, rod-shaped one is a bacillus. If a bacillus is curved, it is a vibrio. A

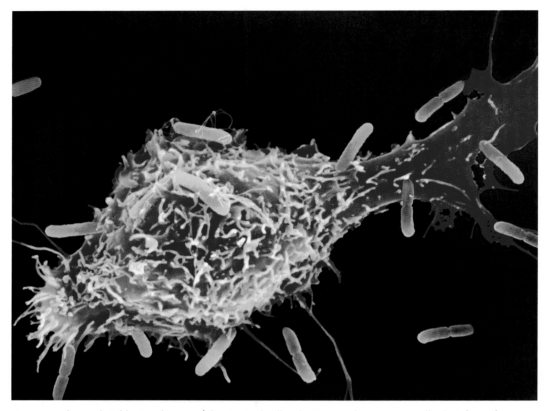

A macrophage (pink) attacks *E. coli* bacteria (yellow). Macrophages are cells that form from white blood cells inside an animal's tissues. They absorb and destroy bacteria and other cells that may be harmful to the host.

spirochete is a flexible, spiral-shaped bacterium. Some bacteria take the form of fine, threadlike shapes called hyphae. Bacteria of many species often form chains or clusters of cells touching each other. Each bacterium in one of these groups, however, is a separate organism.

Many bacteria of different species look alike. Even within a single species, bacteria can vary somewhat in both size and shape. For these reasons scientists cannot usually identify a bacterium's species simply by

BACTERIAL FORMS

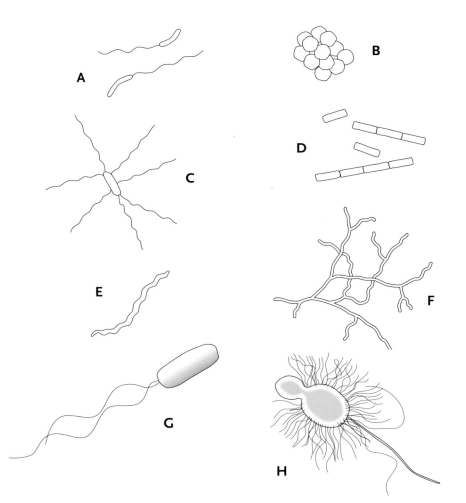

Bacteriologists sometimes group monerans into categories based on shape. *Vibrio cholerae* (A), which causes the disease cholera, is a vibrio or curved bacillus. Cocci such as *Staphylococcus aureus* (B) often form clusters. Rod-shaped bacilla such as *Escherichia coli* (C) may have flagella. Like *Bacillus anthracis* (D), the source of anthrax, some bacteria form chains. Flexible or spiral cells such as *Treponema pallidum* (E) are spirochetes. *Streptomyces albans* (F) takes the form of hyphae, or branching threads. *Rhizobium leguminosarum* (G) is a rod-shaped, soil-dwelling bacterium with one or two flagella, while the aquatic *Planctomyces maris* (H) moves through the water with the help of many flagella.

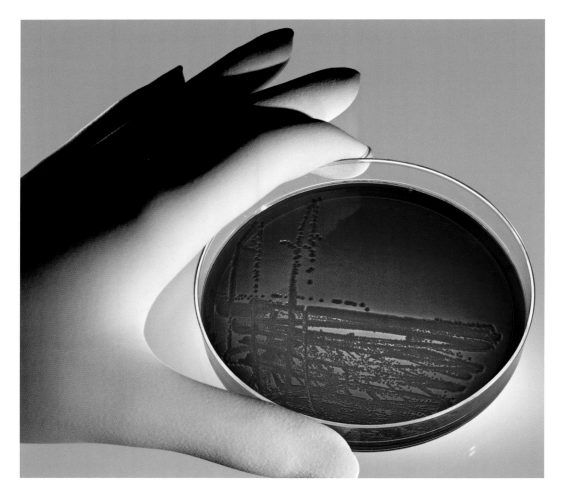

A laboratory technician holds a petri dish in which a bacterial colony has been cultured. A stain test shows that the microbes are coliform bacteria, which can be a sign of unsanitary food or water.

looking at the bacterium through a microscope. They rely on an array of observations and tests to identify bacteria.

The traditional method of identifying bacteria starts with culturing microbes, or growing bacterial colonies. The bacteriologist places a bacterium—or, more often, a sample of soil, water, infected tissue, or other material that contains bacteria—in a sterile container of a nutrient called agar. Agar is a type of alga that nourishes bacterial growth, and then keeps it warm. In this ideal environment, each species of bacterium in the sample will multiply into a colony with plenty of cells for the bacteriologist to observe, compare with known samples, and test.

The bacteriologist may start by observing the sample's reaction to certain chemical stains, its movements, its growth rate, and its ability to produce chemicals called enzymes as part of its life cycle. There are dozens of specific chemical tests that can quickly identify certain disease-causing microbes.

Bacteriologists also apply DNA-based tests to microbes. These tests analyze the genetic material contained inside bacteria. Such tests have two general uses. One use is to detect and identify the bacteria that are responsible for specific medical or environmental conditions. The other is to find new species of bacteria and classify them. The advantage of DNA-based tests is that they can be performed directly on samples of soil, tissue, and other materials, without the need for growing the bacteria in pure cultures.

The 2007 edition of the Taxonomic Outline of Bacteria and Archaea (TOBA) lists more than 8,200 species of prokaryotes that have been identified and classified according to their genetic structures. Microbiologists know, however, that these are just a tiny fraction of the prokaryote species that exist in the world. One 2002 study estimated the total number of prokaryote species as a billion. Although science may never identify every species, DNA-based testing of microbes is getting easier and faster all the time. With microbe hunters seeking out new species for taxonomic, medical, and industrial purposes, the catalog of known bacteria and archaea gets longer every day.

A sterile laboratory bench is the setting for work on bacterial cultures, which must be protected from contamination.

Microbiologists group bacteria into categories, usually called phyla. The number of these phyla, and their names, varies from one expert to another because microbiologists have proposed several different taxonomies for the prokaryotes. Most experts, though, follow a system much like the one used by TOBA, which recognizes twenty-five phyla of bacteria.

Some phyla are better known, or have more named representatives, than others. Bacteriologists have studied many members of the spirochete phylum, for example, because bacteria in this group are responsible for a number of human diseases, including syphilis, yaws, and leptospirosis. The firmicute phylum also contains a number of pathogens, or disease-causing microbes, including the *Staphylococcus* and *Streptococcus* genera, which cause many infectious diseases, some of them severe; *Bacillus cereus*, which causes food poisoning; and the genus *Clostridium*, responsible for botulism and tetanus. On the other hand, the actinobacteria phylum contains the genus

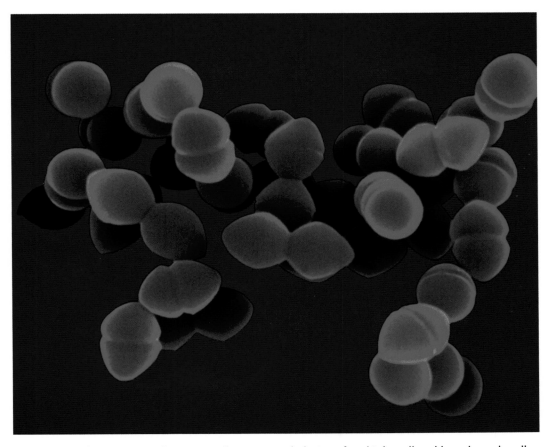

Streptococcus bacteria usually occur in long, twisted chains of multiple cells, although each cell is an independent organism.

Streptomyces, bacteria that produce chemical compounds used as antibiotics—weapons against other, harmful bacteria. *Streptomyces* bacteria are the source of streptomycin, neomycin, tetracycline, and other medications used to treat bacterial infections.

The cyanobacteria are an important phylum of bacterial photosynthesizers, producing food and energy from sunlight, water, and carbon dioxide. Like other photosynthesizers, cyanobacteria capture energy from

Proteins called phycobilisomes give a blue-green color to most cyanobacteria. The phycobilisomes play a role in photosynthesis, which turns the energy from sunlight into food energy.

sunlight and make it available to other forms of life that eat the photosynthesizers. As a byproduct of this process they release oxygen into Earth's atmosphere. Found in most water and soil, cyanobacteria also support plant life by acting as nitrogen-fixers. They absorb nitrogen in the form of gas from the atmosphere and turn it into nitrogen-rich chemical compounds in the water and soil. These compounds provide vital nutrients for plants (fertilizer, which helps plants grow, is mostly nitrogen).

THE STRUCTURE OF A BACTERIUM

At the center of every prokaryote is its genetic material: a chromosome, which is a loop or string of DNA that is made up of genes. (Some bacteria contain more than one copy of the chromosome.) The chromosome is sometimes longer than the cell. An *Escherichia coli,* or *E. coli* bacterium that is just 3 or 4 micrometers long, for example, may contain a chromosome that is 1.3 mm long. The chromosome fits into the cell because it is tightly folded.

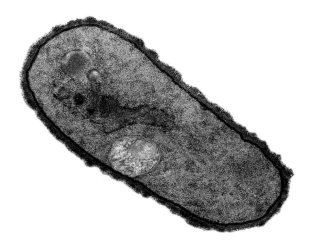

Each bacterium's chromosome is curled, bunched, or folded into a mass called the nucleoid. In a eukaryotic cell, a membrane would encase the nucleoid, forming the cell nucleus. But in the prokaryotic cell, the nucleoid simply floats in the cytoplasm, a watery liquid that fills the cell. The nucleoid is not the

Bacillus megaterium is a typical moneran, or cell without a nucleus. Within its cytoplasm float a nucleoid (dark blue) and a storage granule (pink). The light blue structure is a mesosome, found only in bacteria that have been chemically treated for viewing through microscopes.

only thing contained in the cytoplasm. Bacteria vary widely in the organization of their cells, and some have more features than others. Most bacteria, however, have certain basic elements. Ribosomes, for example, are found in the cytoplasm of all cells, both prokaryotic and eukaryotic, although prokaryotes' ribosomes are smaller.

Ribosomes are sites in the cytoplasm where the information contained in the cell's DNA is translated into proteins. The ribosomes consist of small, rounded bundles of protein and RNA, which is the genetic material that decodes the DNA and turns that information into specific proteins. One gene of ribosomal RNA, called 16S rRNA, was the key to identifying the archaea. Scientists now use this gene to classify prokaryotes.

Storage granules may also be found in a bacterium's cytoplasm. These are packets of nutrients that the cell is holding in reserve. In addition, some water-dwelling bacteria and archaea contain hollow bubbles called gas vacuoles. These determine how buoyant a free-floating cell will be. The

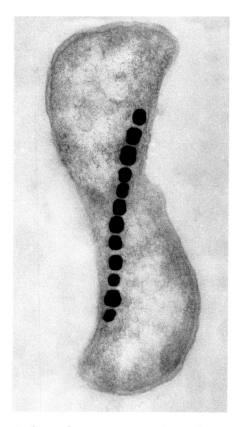

A chain of magnetite particles makes this *Magnetospirillum* bacterium line up with the earth's magnetic fields. Scientists do not yet know why these bacteria, discovered in 1975, are magnetized.

more gas vacuoles the cell has, the higher it will float in the water, and the more light it will receive. The gas vacuoles form when the cell is low in the water. They cause the cell to rise. The vacuoles then gradually shrink or disappear. As the vacuoles disappear, the cell sinks. Soon new vacuoles form, starting the cycle again.

Particles of magnetite, a magnetic mineral, are held in the cytoplasm of some aquatic bacteria, including the genus *Magnetospirillum.* These particles make the bacteria line up with magnetic fields, although scientists do not know what purpose this serves. Bacteria can also contain crystals of various chemical compounds. Scientists have found that crystals inside *Bacillus thuringiensis,* for example, are poisonous to certain insects, which has led farmers to use this bacterium against crop-devouring pests.

The cytoplasm and all its contents are enclosed in the cell envelope, which is the microbe's "skin," separating it from the outside world. The cell envelope has two layers. The inner layer, next to the cytoplasm, is a sac or film called the cytoplasmic membrane. The outer layer is the cell wall, a mesh-like shell that protects and supports the cell contents while letting nutrients and waste products pass in and out of the cell.

Cell walls of bacteria are made of peptidoglycan, a mixture of sugars and amino acids. There are two main types of cell walls, Gram-negative and Gram-positive. (The names refer to how the bacteria react to a staining

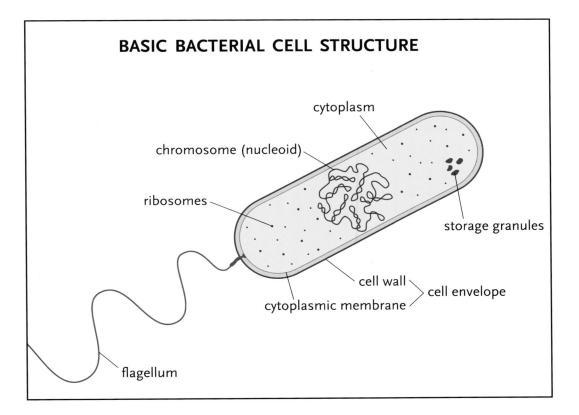

BASIC BACTERIAL CELL STRUCTURE

cytoplasm

chromosome (nucleoid)

ribosomes

storage granules

cell wall

cell envelope

cytoplasmic membrane

flagellum

process that a Danish scientist named Christian Gram developed in the 1880s.) Gram-positive walls are thicker and smoother than Gram-negative walls.

Bacteria sometimes form additional layers on their outer surfaces by secreting proteins through the cell walls. A slime layer is a watery film that helps bacteria stick together. A capsule is a thicker and tougher covering. Like slime layers, capsules help bacteria stick to one another, but in addition they protect bacterial cells from drying out or from being attacked by viruses. A capsule can also serve as a storage unit for reserve nutrients.

Even sturdier than capsules are endospores, protective structures that form inside a few varieties of bacteria when conditions in the environment become hostile. In a process called sporulation, a bacterium produces a copy of its own DNA and then encloses that copy in a shell made of several layers of peptidoglycan and calcium. When the bacteria dies, the endospore remains—not dead, not growing, but dormant, like a hibernating animal. An endospore can survive all kinds of stresses, including radiation, extreme temperatures, lack of nutrition and water, even the airlessness of space. It can remain in a kind of suspended animation for millions of years, if necessary. When the endospore encounters favorable conditions, its protective coating splits apart or dissolves, and the bacterium comes back to life, ready to grow and multiply.

Myxobacteria, sometimes called slime bacteria, follow a similar strategy when environmental conditions become difficult, or nutrients become scarce. They form clusters called fruiting bodies, with each bacterium encased in a tough shell called a myxospore. In this way the myxobacteria wait out the hard times. When conditions are right, the shells dissolve and the bacteria start growing again, not as isolated individuals but in a swarm. Being in a swarm is a good start for a growing myxobacterium. These microbes produce digestive chemicals called enzymes that pass out

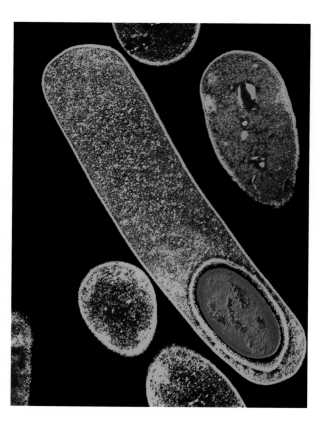

An endospore (red) is forming within a *Clostridium difficile* bacterium. *C. difficile* can cause dangerous diarrhea in humans and is hard to treat because its sturdy endospores resist antibiotics.

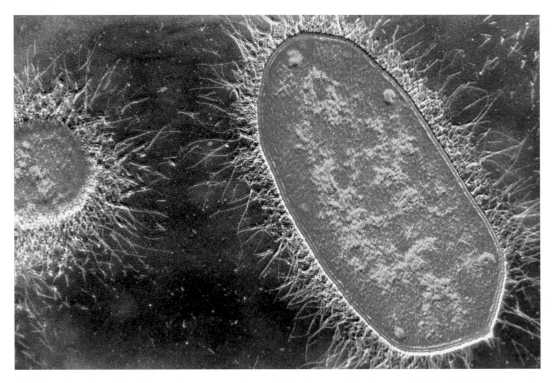

The fine, hairlike growths on the outer surface of this bacterial cell are pili. The pili help bacteria stick to other bacteria and also to different kinds of cells, such as the tissues of infected hosts.

through their cell walls. A swarm produces enough enzymes to help all of its members absorb and break down nutrients.

Many bacteria have outgrowths that look like tiny tails or hairs. There are three types of outgrowths: pili, fimbria, and flagella. Pili are hairs or spikes of protein that stick up from the outer cell walls of certain types of Gram-negative bacteria. These bacteria can exchange DNA among themselves through direct contact, and the exchange takes place through the pili. Fimbria are thin rods of protein, smaller than pili. Scientists think that their purpose is to help bacteria attach themselves to other bacteria or to solid surfaces.

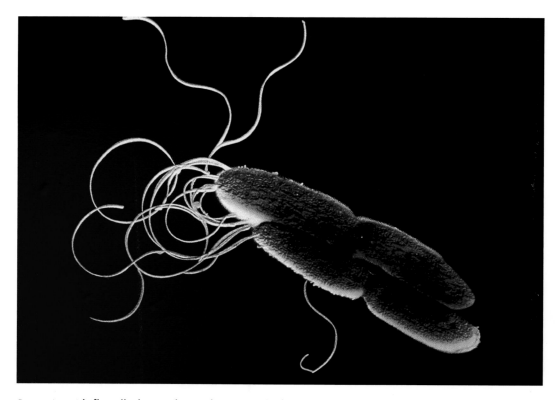

Bacteria with flagella located at only one end of the cell can move in just a single direction, but they can move through liquid at speeds of up to sixty times their own length per second.

Flagella are long, whiplike tubes made of protein. Depending upon the species, a bacterium may have one flagellum or many, or none. Species that have flagella use them to swim through liquids. A flagellum rotates along its length, like a screwdriver being turned. The energy that turns the flagellum comes from the movement of particles such as hydrogen ions as they flow across membranes, pulled by the weak electrical attractions that occur naturally among such particles. The energy from this movement is transferred to the flagellum through a complex arrangement of protein structures that works like a microscopically small motor set in the bacterium's cell envelope. As the flagellum rotates, it pushes the bacterium forward.

Bacteria with flagella are not the only ones that have motility, which is the scientific term for the power to move. A few varieties of bacteria can move without flagella. Scientists call their movements gliding motility and twitching motility. They do not yet know exactly how these movements take place. There may be several different mechanisms for movement. Some seem to involve pili and fimbria. Others may involve tiny "jets" that squirt matter out of the cell, or wavelike motions of the cell envelope. Motility without flagella has been observed in cyanobacteria and myxobacteria, among others. Myxobacteria move both as individual cells and as swarms or groups of cells. Microbiologists call these types of movement "adventurous" and "social" motility.

THE LIVES OF BACTERIA

Metabolism

Every living thing has a metabolism, a way of getting the energy and nutrients it needs to live. The organism's method of getting and using energy is called its metabolic pathway. Bacteria and archaea have a greater variety of metabolic pathways than eukaryotic organisms. In other words, bacteria have many different ways of feeding, and many different food sources.

An organism requires both energy and raw materials such as carbon for building cells. Living things that get their raw materials from one source and their energy from another source are called autotrophs. A plant is an autotroph. It gets energy from sunlight and nutrients from the soil, water, and air (taking carbon dioxide from the atmosphere). Organisms that get raw materials and energy from the same source are called heterotrophs. Animals, including people, are heterotrophs. Their food provides both raw materials and energy, which is released during the chemical processes of digestion.

Bacteriologists have identified four main metabolic pathways in the

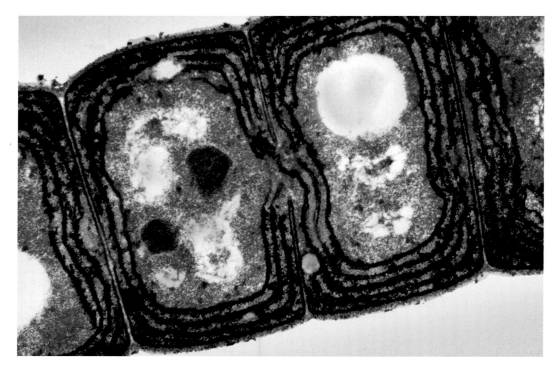

Cyanobacteria or blue-green algae are photoautotrophs, organisms that get their energy from sunlight through photosynthesis and release oxygen as a byproduct. They can get the carbon they need for photosynthesis either from the air or from their surroundings, which means that their metabolisms can operate both aerobically and anaerobically (with or without air).

bacterial domain, based on how the bacteria get energy and carbon. Photoautotrophs (also known as photosynthesizers) get energy from sunlight and carbon from the atmosphere. Photoheterotrophs also get energy from sunlight, but their carbon comes from chemical compounds in their environments, which can vary from the roots of plants to human and animal intestines. Chemoheterotrophs get their energy as well as their carbon from the organic (carbon-containing) compounds they absorb, just as animals and fungi do. Many of the best-known bacteria belong to this group because chemoheterotrophic bacteria are easier to culture and study in laboratories than the other metabolic varieties.

The fourth metabolic category is found nowhere else but in prokaryotes. Chemoautotrophs, like photosynthesizers, get carbon from carbon dioxide in the atmosphere. Their energy, however, comes from reacting with inorganic chemicals in their environments. Depending upon the species, energy sources include sulfur, hydrogen, iron, nitrogen compounds, and more. No eukaryotic organisms are known to take energy directly from minerals and other inorganic sources.

Rhizobium leguminosarum is an agriculturally important bacterium. Living in soil and plant roots, it is a nitrogen fixer, breaking down nitrogen from the atmosphere into a form that plants can absorb.

Chemoautotrophs can grow without any light at all, as long as they have access to carbon dioxide and the necessary minerals. Researchers have found such bacteria growing in cracks or pores in rock deep underground, or inside stone statues, slowly eating away at the minerals. Such bacteria are sometimes called chemolithotrophs, from the Greek word *lithos*, meaning rock. They can live and multiply in places that would have been considered utterly hostile to life just half a century ago.

Another way of categorizing bacteria has to do with oxygen. Aerobic bacteria use oxygen to oxidize, or break down, molecules as part of the metabolic process. Anaerobic bacteria use other chemical compounds, such as sulfate or carbon dioxide, in their chemical reaction. Oxygen is toxic to most anaerobic microbes. Between these two extremes are the microaerophiles. They use oxygen in small amounts but cannot tolerate large amounts of it.

Reproduction

In contrast to their wide variety of metabolic pathways, prokaryotes have just one basic way of reproducing. It is called binary fission, or cell division. The process begins with DNA replication. The chromosome or chain of DNA in the center of the bacterium replicates, or makes a copy of itself. When there are two complete sets of DNA, they separate. The bacterium stretches, and a membrane forms across the middle of it. Then, in a process called cytokinesis, the cell envelope grows inward along the membrane until it splits the cell into two daughter cells. Each of them is a clone of the original cell, with the original cell's DNA. When conditions are favorable, with plenty of nutrients, bacteria can divide every twelve to twenty minutes. Each time they divide, their numbers double, which allows bacterial populations to grow extremely fast.

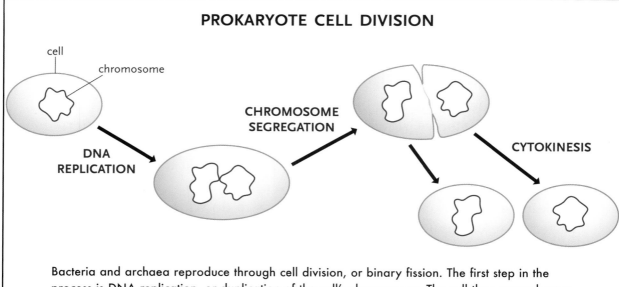

PROKARYOTE CELL DIVISION

cell

chromosome

CHROMOSOME SEGREGATION

DNA REPLICATION

CYTOKINESIS

Bacteria and archaea reproduce through cell division, or binary fission. The first step in the process is DNA replication, or duplication of the cell's chromosome. The cell then grows longer, which causes a segregation or separation between the original and the replicated chromosomes. In the third step, cytokinesis, a membrane divides the cell into two parts. Reproduction is complete when they separate into two daughter cells.

Bacteria do not always split neatly in two. Sometimes, in a process called budding, a small projection juts out from the main part of the cell. This bud contains the duplicate chromosome. The stem connecting the bud to the parent cell shrinks until the bud is pinched off as an independent cell, which then grows to normal size.

There are no male or female prokaryotes. Cell division is an asexual form of reproduction, without gender and without the mingling of genetic material from different parents. Yet changes do occur in the genetic material of bacteria. DNA replication does not always work perfectly. Sometimes errors occur in the copying process, creating mutations. Radiation and certain chemicals can also disrupt DNA, giving rise to mutations that are passed on through cell division.

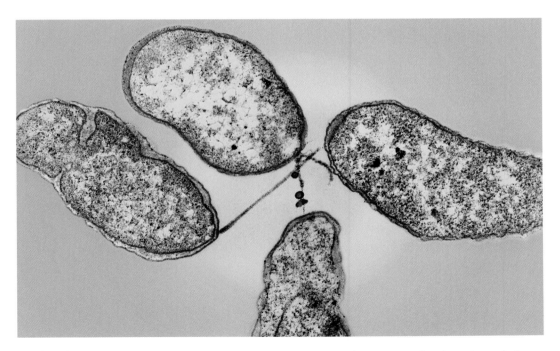

Cholera bacteria are conjugating, or passing genetic material among each other along their pili. Although scientists once thought that bacteria reproduced only asexually, conjugation is a form of sexual reproduction because it mingles DNA from different organisms.

Bacterial Battleground

Bacteria can be tough enough to eat stone, but they have enemies. "Every two days, half the bacteria on Earth are killed," says Vincent Fischetti, head of a bacterial research laboratory at New York's Rockefeller University. The killers are viruses known as bacteriophages, or bacteria-eaters. Scientists call them phages for short.

Unlike the viruses that cause AIDS, influenza, the common cold, and a host of other health problems for humans, bacteriophages do not harm people. They are deadly to bacteria, though. The viruses do not really eat the bacteria—in fact, scientists don't think viruses eat at all. Scientists debate whether viruses, which cannot reproduce on their own, can even be considered to be alive. Viruses reproduce by taking over the genetic material of other organisms. That's how phages destroy bacteria. They break through the cell walls, take control of the DNA of the bacteria, and use it to make copies of themselves. The bacteria die, and the viruses are released to go out and repeat the process.

Phages are smaller than bacteria but a lot more numerous. There may be ten times as many phages as bacteria in the world. But although phages kill vast numbers of bacteria, the bacteria manage to hold their own because they multiply quickly and often. But although phages cannot wipe out bacteria worldwide, they win many smaller battles.

Doctors in the early twentieth century experimented with using phages to kill the bacteria that had infected their patients. After

In this computer-generated artwork, phages explode out of a bacterium they have destroyed. These phages have twenty-sided heads and tails with bent fibers that inject the phages' genetic material into bacteria. After multiplying inside a bacterium, the phages burst out, rupturing and killing the bacterial cell.

antibiotic drugs were discovered in the mid-twentieth century, interest in the medical use of phages died away. Phages are now a hot topic of research, however, because many strains of bacteria have developed resistance to antibiotics. Possible uses for phages range from cleaning infected wounds to sterilizing food to controlling agricultural pests. These little viruses may turn out to be vital allies in humankind's long war against destructive bacteria.

Bacteria can also acquire DNA from outside sources, through genetic transfer. They exchange sections of DNA called plasmids with other bacteria through direct contact, using their pili to pass the genetic material (this type of genetic transfer is as close to sexual reproduction as bacteria get). Bacteria can also absorb stray plasmids that happen to be floating around in their environments. Finally, viruses called bacteriophages burrow into bacteria. Occasionally a virus carries part of one bacterium's DNA into another bacterium, where it attaches to the new host's chromosome.

Because bacterial DNA can be altered in so many ways, bacterial species change, evolve, and adapt to new circumstances, sometimes quite quickly. For example, they acquire resistance to medications used against them. The genetic changes that occur because of mutation and genetic transfer are random, but any changes that help the bacteria survive will be passed along through cell division. As the population grows, the favorable new features become more and more common.

THE ARCHAEA: EXTREME MONERANS

When the archaea were identified in the late 1970s, people wondered how an entire domain of living things—one of the three main branches of life on Earth—had remained undiscovered until then. One reason is that to a microscopist, archaea look a lot like bacteria. People had previously observed some archaea, but they thought they were looking at bacteria. Now that archaea have been set apart from bacteria, however, scientists are aware of the differences between bacteria and archaea. They know that although both bacteria and archaea are prokaryotes, they are no more closely related to each other than either of them is to eukaryotes.

Scientists use differences in the 16S rRNA gene to tell bacteria and archaea apart, but other differences have to do with chemistry and cell structure. A bacterium's cell membrane contains chemicals called esters. In an archaeon's cell membrane, the same function is filled by chemicals

Methanosarcina mazei is one of many archaea that form methane gas as byproducts of their metabolism.

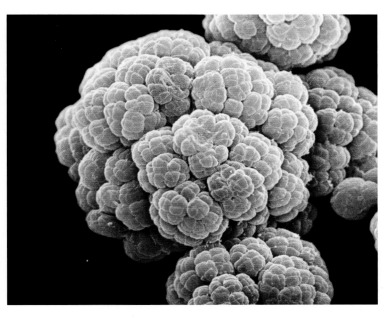

called ethers. The compound pepti-doglycan, found in the cell walls of bacteria, does not occur in archaea, although their cell walls sometimes contain a similar compound called pseudomurein. The two groups' flagella are different, too. When archaea have flagella, they are thinner than those of bacteria. Microbiologists think that archaeal flagella grow outward from the base, while bacterial flagella grow at the tip.

More general differences exist between the two domains. Although photosynthesis occurs in at least five phyla of bacteria, for example, no known archaea are photosynthesizers. On the other hand, no known bacteria are methanogens, or methane-formers, while many archaea, including the first archaeon ever identified, are methanogens. A difference that is particularly important to human beings is that all the prokaryotes that are pathogens, or sources of disease, are bacteria. No archaeal pathogens are known. These differences may become blurred as scientists learn more about the archaea. They may discover species that photosynthesize, or that cause diseases.

One difference between bacteria and archaea has already become blurred. When scientists discovered the archaea, these microorganisms were found in environments or conditions that seemed inhospitable to life—places like hot springs, bone-dry deserts, polar ice, and highly acidic

Once thought to live only in extreme environments, archaea are found in many ordinary places, such as common garden soil.

or salty water and soil. Scientists called the archaea extremophiles (lovers of extremes) because of their ability not just to survive but to thrive in these extreme habitats.

However, since that time, researchers have learned that not all archaea are extremophiles. Many archaea do live in extreme habitats, but archaea have been found in great numbers in non-extreme habitats, such as ordinary soil. They have also turned up in plankton, the masses of microorganisms drifting in the world's oceans. The archaea that do not live in or require extreme conditions are known as mesophiles (lovers of the middle).

Just as not all archaea are extremophiles, not all extremophiles are archaea. Insects, worms, shrimp, and the tiny insect-like animals known as tardigrades have all been found living in extreme conditions. A number of bacteria are extremophiles as well.

Extremophile monerans (bacteria and archaea) come in many varieties. There are thermophiles, or heat-lovers, that live in waters of hot springs and undersea vents, where temperatures reach 140 to 176 degrees Fahrenheit (60 to 80 degrees Celsius). *Thermotoga maritima,* for example, is a thermophilic bacterium first found in hot mud on the sea bottom near the volcanic island of Vulcano, Italy (the source of the word "volcano"). *T. maritima* is especially interesting to microbiologists because, although it is a bacterium, it has some genetic similarities to the archaea. It may be the closest living relative of an ancient microbe that was the ancestor of both bacteria and archaea. *T. maritima* grows best at around 176 °F (80 °C), but some archaea like it even hotter. Known as hyperthermophiles, they live in water with temperatures up to and above the boiling point of water, 212 °F (100 °C).

Halophiles live in water that is saltier than normal seawater. Acidophiles and alkaliphiles live in water that is significantly more or less acidic than average. Some microorganisms are extremophiles in more than one way. Microbes that tolerate both high heat and high levels of minerals,

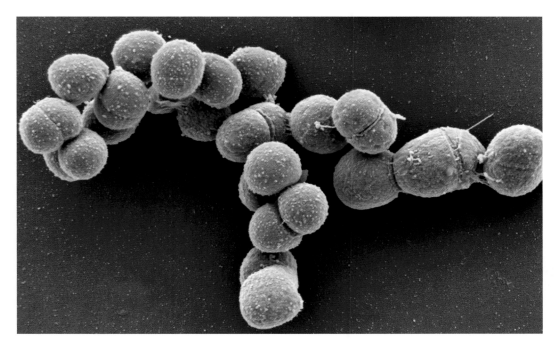

Halophiles, or salt-tolerant bacteria such as these, live in water with high concentrations of mineral salts that would be toxic to many other forms of life.

for example, are found in hot sulfur springs like those of Yellowstone National Park. Large colonies or mats of these microorganisms give such springs their characteristic colors.

Bacteria and archaea have colonized other extreme environments as well. Endoliths occupy microscopically small pores in rock. These microbes play an important role in the breaking down of bedrock into grains of sand and dirt. Cryophiles flourish in cold habitats, such as permafrost, ice, and snow, with temperatures below the freezing point of water, 32 °F (0 °C). Xerophiles live in very dry environments such as desert soils. Piezophiles, which tolerate high pressure, can live at great depths underground or in undersea trenches. Radioresistant microbes are unaffected by radiation, while metalotolerant ones can live in liquids that contain high concentrations of toxic minerals such as arsenic.

The taxonomy of the archaea is even less settled than that of the bacteria, because fewer archaea are known and they have not been studied for long. The Taxonomic Outline of Bacteria and Archaea (TOBA) recognizes just two phyla of archaea, the euryarchaeotes and the crenarchaeotes, which are identified by genetic differences in their ribosomal RNA. The euryarchaeote phylum contains the methane producers, the halophilic archaea, and many of the thermophiles and hyperthermophiles. Thermophiles and hyperthermophiles are found among the crenarchaeotes as well, but that the phylum also contains the archaea that are found in plankton throughout the oceans.

Obsidian Pool is a dark, steaming hot spring in Yellowstone National Park. In the 1990s, while examining samples from Obsidian Pool, researchers found sequences of ribosomal RNA from an unknown type of archaeon, neither a euryarchaeote nor a crenarchaeote. Since that time, similar pieces of genetic material have turned up in water from hot springs and hot undersea vents. For now, this material has been assigned to a third phylum of archaea called the korarchaeotes. Scientists do not yet know anything about the achaea in this phylum, however, because they have not yet managed to isolate and grow korarcheotes in pure laboratory cultures.

Since the 1970s, scientists have found many species of archaea living in the hot, mineral-rich springs of Yellowstone National Park. Many of the discoveries took place here, in the dark, bubbling waters of Obsidian Pool.

LIFE ON EARTH AND ELSEWHERE

Pyrococcus abyssi is one tough microbe. The name of this archaeon describes the extreme environments it inhabits—*pyro* means "having to do with fire," and *abyssi* means "of great depths." *P. abyssi* was first isolated from a black smoker—a vent spewing hot, mineral-filled water—on the floor of the Pacific Ocean at a depth of 11,500 feet (3,500 meters). Researchers have found that *P. abyssi* grows best in water that is at the boiling point, and at pressures 200 times greater than on the Earth's surface.

In 1999 researchers decoded *P. abyssi*'s entire genome (genetic blueprint), about 1.7 million units of DNA. The genomes of extremophiles such as *P. abyssi* interest scientists for several reasons. Extremophiles and the chemicals they produce have industrial, medical, and commercial uses. Enzymes made by extremophiles, for example, can survive in environments such as acidic stomach fluids, alkaline detergents, and high-temperature water or industrial processes. Such enzymes are already used as additives in animal feed and laundry detergent. They are also important in certain high-temperature medical and scientific techniques, such as DNA testing and cancer screening. New information about extremophiles may lead to additional products and uses.

Astrobiologists love extremophiles, too. Astrobiology is the branch of science concerned with life on other worlds. (At this time it is a science of theories, because no solid evidence of life beyond Earth has yet been found.) One of astrobiologists' chief concerns is defining the conditions in which life could exist, and the discovery of extremophiles dramatically broadened those conditions. Astrobiologists have joined microbiologists to search for and study extremophiles that live in conditions like those that may exist on other planets or their moons. If there is life on these worlds, it may take the form of microbes adapted to extreme conditions.

Based on what is known about extremophiles and about other bodies in the solar system, many astrobiologists think that the likeliest places to find life are the planet Mars and Europa, a moon of Jupiter. Water, which is necessary for all life on Earth, exists on Mars and probably exists on Europa. Two of Saturn's moons, Titan and Enceladus, may also be home to extraterrestrial life. Enceladus may have an ocean under its covering of ice, and Titan is known to have liquid oceans (although they are made of methane and ethane, not water).

Some earthly microbes can endure extremes of cold and radiation, which are characteristics of space. In the form of endospores, they can remain dormant for long periods time—perhaps long enough to travel from one world or solar system to the next. A few astrobiologists have

Astrobiologist Lynn J. Rothschild takes a sample from a microbial mat in a lake. Researchers wonder whether microbes that can endure extreme conditions on Earth could survive the harsher conditions of space.

speculated about panspermia, the idea that life can be carried through space by asteroids, comets, or solar winds. Perhaps one day they will discover that life on Earth originated elsewhere—or that earthly life, in the form of microbial endospores, has colonized other worlds.

If panspermia is an idea on the fringe of science, the origin of life on Earth is a primary goal of research for many scientists. Their current knowledge and theories about the beginning of life on this planet owe much to the bacteria and archaea.

Physical evidence of ancient life comes in the form of fossils, preserved remains or traces of living things. Fossils of monerans are rare, because organisms that are small and soft do not fossilize well. Still, some traces remain of microorganisms that lived long ago. Two-billion-year-old rocks contain tiny crystals of magnetite like those found in some species of bacteria today. Endoliths, bacteria that gnaw miscroscopic channels through rock, have left trails in ancient stone.

Occasionally, bacterial cells are filled in or coated by minerals such as iron compounds that preserve the shapes of the bacteria in rock. These microscopic traces are called pseudomorphs. It can be very difficult to tell pseudomorphs from other kinds of formations that occur in rock. Meteorite ALH84001 is a chunk of Martian rock that landed on Earth in Antarctica. Some scientists experts think that this rock contains pseudomorphs, evidence that bacterial life once existed on Mars. Others say that the structures in the meteorite can be explained in different ways, so the rock cannot stand as proof of Martian life.

ALH84001 remains open to question, but other traces of ancient bacterial life are unmistakable. They are fossils of cyanobacteria. Cyanobacteria are good candidates for fossilization for several reasons. First, they are larger than many other bacteria, with thick cell walls. Second, they often group together in vast numbers, forming bacterial mats. Over time, the mats produce structures called stromatolites.

As cyanobacteria grow, they produce calcium carbonate as a byproduct of photosynthesis. (Calcium carbonate is a key element in limestone, a type of soft rock.) While cyanobacteria build up in layer upon layer, the calcium carbonate they give off hardens around particles of alga, sand, and other debris. The result is a stromatolite, a stony growth with a living mat of cyanobacteria on top. Most stromatolites are round, dome-shaped, or mushroom-shaped.

Stromatolites are rare in the modern world. They form only in a few lakes and lagoons that are too salty for animal life; in other places, microorganisms and other animals eat the bacteria, preventing stromatolites from forming. Shark Bay in Western Australia and Lagoa Salgada in Brazil are two sites with modern stromatolites that scientists have studied. Scientists have also found fossils of very old stromatolites, which were numerous in

Hamelin Pool Marine Nature Reserve in Western Australia's Shark Bay is one of the few places in the world where you can see stromatolites. These hard, lumpy growths formed and covered by mats of algae were common in the shallow seas billions of years ago.

the world's warm, shallow waters for millions and millions of years. Inside some of these fossilized stromatolites they have found the remains of ancient bacterial life. The oldest known fossils in the world are microbes much like modern cyanobacteria. They are 3.5 billion years old.

The Earth itself is about 4.5 billion years old. One billion years after the Earth formed from a cloud of matter orbiting the sun, it was teeming with bacterial life. Scientists do not yet know when life first appeared, or how, or whether bacteria were the first life forms. They think, however, that conditions on the young Earth were a lot like conditions in hot springs and

Hot, sulfur-filled liquid pours out of a black smoker, a vent located on the floor of the Atlantic Ocean. Crabs, shrimp, worms, and many types of monerans thrive in this seemingly inhospitable environment.

black smokers today: no oxygen, high temperatures, lots of sulfur and salt. Prokaryotic extremophiles live in those conditions today. The first life forms could have resembled them.

Carl Woese, the discoverer of the archaea, thought that all three domains—archaea, bacteria, and eukaryota—might have descended from the same original ancestor. He called this ancestor a progenote, but no evidence of it has been found. Another possibility is that the archaea were the first life forms, and that both bacteria and eukaryotes evolved from them. Recent genetic studies of the archaea seem to support this theory. Some biologists, however, think that both the archaea and the eukaryota evolved

Myvatn, a shallow lake in a geothermally active part of northern Iceland, is known for its high concentrations of algae and other bacteria.

from ancestral bacteria. Or perhaps the archaea evolved from bacteria, and the eukaryota were formed when a bacterium absorbed an archaeon, which took on the role of a cell nucleus.

Only further research, and perhaps the discovery of still more ancient fossil microbes, will untangle the roots of the tree of life. Still, the general outline of its three branches is clear. Monerans, the smallest microorganisms, fill two of those three branches.

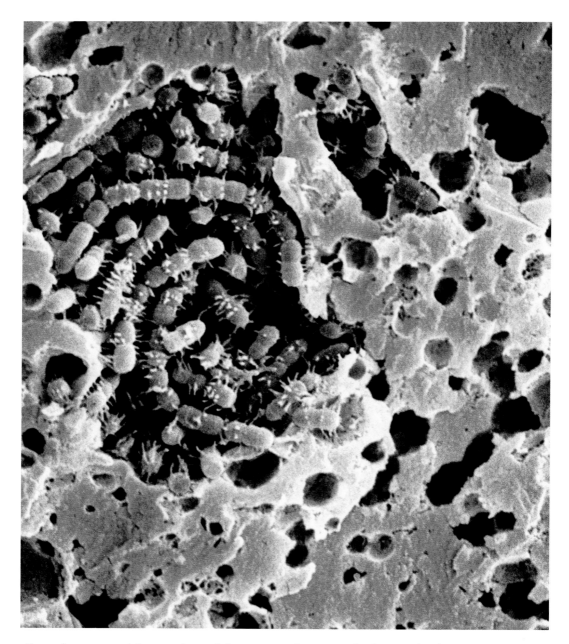

Goat cheese containing a colony of *Streptococcus* bacteria. This bacterial culture is not an invader—the cheese makers used it to make the milk thicken into cheese.

Living with Monerans

"The unseen majority" is how a 1998 article in the *Proceedings of the National Academy of Sciences* described the bacteria and archaea. These prokaryotes, or monerans, are truly unseen by ordinary sight, unless vast numbers of them cluster together to form mats or films. They also make up the majority of all life on the planet.

Scientists estimate that a third of an ounce of typical soil (about 28 grams) contains 40 million prokaryotes. The estimated total of prokaryotes in the world is a number so large that only a mathematician can imagine it: a five with thirty zeroes after it. And that may be an underestimate.

Prokaryotes were around long before humans appeared on Earth, and they may well outlive humans and most other life forms as well. People, like all other organisms, have had to adapt to living in a world full of bacteria. One of the most significant advances in the history of medicine came when scientists realized that bacteria are more than tiny curiosities—they cause many of our most troublesome diseases. Yet scientists have also learned that without bacteria, humans would not survive.

BACTERIA IN COMMUNITIES

Bacteria are individual organisms, but they do not live in isolation. They exist in a network of relationships with the organisms around them, including other bacteria. Sometimes bacteria simply stick together. Millions of members of the same species of bacteria may adhere to one another, forming mats or films that are visible to ordinary sight. Another visible phenomenon is the bloom—a sudden, dramatic increase in the number of microorganisms in water, usually because of favorable conditions such as warmth, or perhaps fertilizer or sewage entering the water. Blooms may consist of various microorganisms, eukaryotes as well as prokaryotes, but often they involve cyanobacteria.

Rock walls are covered with mats of bacteria in the Valley of the Geysers in eastern Russia. Although such mats contain trillions of bacterial cells that have stuck together, each cell is a complete organism that could live on its own.

The pinecone fish is one of many marine species that glow because bacteria living in their organs give off light.

Some species of bacteria behave differently at high density (when they are concentrated in large numbers) than when their density is low. *Vibrio fischeri*, for example, can live in two ways: as a free-living microorganism in the ocean, or at high density inside the light organs of certain fish. As a free-living bacterium, *V. fischeri* does not produce light. At high densities, however, special genes in the bacteria are activated, producing a blue-green light that gives the light organs of certain undersea creatures their luminous glow.

How does *V. fischeri* know to "turn on" its light genes? The answer is a kind of molecular communication that microbiologists call quorum sensing. The bacteria give off molecules that act as signals. If population density is low, the bacteria ignore each other's signals. When the population reaches a certain density, however, there are enough molecular signals floating around to activate the light-producing genes inside the cells. The level at which the cells are activated is called the quorum; the signal molecules tell the individual bacteria when the quorum has been reached. Activating the light genes is nothing like a conscious decision, however. It is an automatic response programmed into the bacterial genome. Researchers have found versions of quorum sensing in many types of bacteria.

Bacteria have close relationships with organisms of other species, too. Such a relationship is called symbiosis, and there are several forms of it.

Lumps called nodules on the roots of these runner beans contain nitrogen-fixing bacteria that provide the plants with essential nutrients.

Mutualism is a kind of symbiosis in which both partners benefit. This kind of relationship exists between bacteria that produce hydrogen as a byproduct of their metabolisms and archaea that consume hydrogen. The bacteria provide food for the archaea, and the archaea keep the level of hydrogen from getting so high that it harms the bacteria. Nitrogen-fixing bacteria live in mutualistic relationships with plants, either in the soil near the roots or in small growths on the roots. The bacteria make nitrogen from the atmosphere available to the plants, which cannot absorb it directly, while the plants provide food for the bacteria in the form of organic compounds.

The millions of bacteria that live in the mouths, stomachs, and intestines of healthy humans and other animals are mutualists, too. The bacteria benefit from a steady diet of organic compounds that slosh through their environments. At the same time, these "good" bacteria provide services for the host animals: helping them break down and digest food;

Got bacteria? Strains of bacteria that help maintain healthy digestion are found in yogurt and other products.

manufacturing vitamins from chemical building blocks; and preventing harmful bacteria from growing. Certain strains of digestive bacteria are so beneficial that products such as yogurt are advertised as containing them.

From the human point of view, not all bacteria are "good." Some are parasites, living in symbiotic relationships in which they benefit but their hosts are harmed. Not only do bacteria form parasitic relationships with many kinds of organisms, but some bacteria can live only as parasites. *Mycobacterium leprae,* for example, is called an obligate parasite because

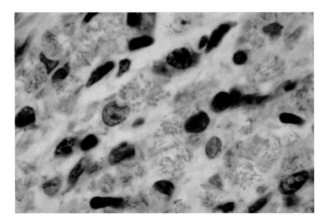

When these bacteria infect human skin and mucous membranes, they live as parasites, destructive to the host. They cause Hansen's disease, or leprosy.

it is required, or obligated, to live inside specific types of cells in eukaryotic host animals. It cannot live in any other environment. Although many bacterial parasites create only annoyance or mild discomfort for their hosts, *M. leprae* is a pathogen—a parasite that brings disease or death. It is the bacterium responsible for leprosy, or Hansen's disease.

GERMS, DISEASE, AND ANTIBIOTICS

For centuries people tried to explain how diseases entered the human body and passed from person to person. As early as the eleventh century, some Arab doctors thought that contagious or infectious diseases were caused by tiny foreign bodies that entered the human body. They also recognized that infection could be passed from person to person on such objects as clothes or drinking cups. In the nineteenth century, European scientists and physicians identified the agents of disease as living microorganisms, which they called germs (scientists today call them pathogens). The germ theory of disease launched a revolution in sanitation and health care.

In the 1850s and 1860s Louis Pasteur, a French chemist who is regarded as one of the founders of microbiology, conducted experiments proving that spoilage, decay, and decomposition in food and other organic materials are caused by airborne microorganisms, both fungi and bacteria. He was one of the inventors of a method for preventing contamination in foods such as milk by using heat to kill microorganisms. Known as pasteurization, that method is still used to ensure food safety today.

Pasteur was convinced that microorganisms also caused disease in animals and people. In the mid-1860s he investigated a disease that was infecting silkworms, threatening the French silk industry. Pasteur traced the source of the disease to specific bacteria. The link between these bacilli and the silkworm infection suggested that the germ theory of disease was correct. Pasteur's findings also suggested that it might be possible to keep people from getting sick by protecting them from germs.

At the time, one of the biggest risks facing hospital patients was infection. A Scottish surgeon named Joseph Lister developed a set of new procedures, such as sterilizing surgical instruments and boiling bed sheets, to destroy germs. Known as antisepsis, these procedures soon became part of medical practice.

With the germ theory of disease firmly established, Pasteur and other researchers worked to identify the specific microorganisms that cause diseases. They found disease-causing viruses as well as bacteria and fungi. The foremost figure in this pioneering work on medical microbiology was a German physician named Robert Koch, who investigated the bacterial causes of three diseases that attack people: cholera, anthrax, and tubercu-

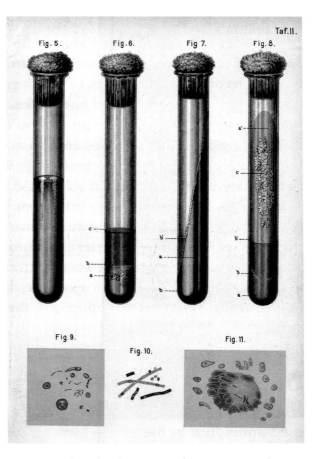

In 1889, when this illustration of pneumonia, tuberculosis, and anthrax bacteria was made, medical researchers were uncovering the links between microbes and disease.

losis. Koch's research on tuberculosis established the germ theory beyond any doubt and produced a set of rules that medical researchers still follow when they want to prove that a particular microorganism causes a particular disease. In 1905 Koch received the Nobel Prize in medicine for his tuberculosis research.

Antisepsis was not the only new development in medicine brought

How Clean is Too Clean?

"Don't touch that! Wash your hands!" Every child hears those instructions over and over. Since scientists found the connection between germs and disease, people have tried to avoid disease by avoiding germs. Hand-washing is one of the best ways to protect yourself against disease-causing bacteria and other pathogens. What could be wrong with that?

Doctors certainly do not want people to stop washing their hands—in fact, doctors know that most people don't wash their hands as often as they should. Yet some doctors and scientists are starting to think that the emphasis on hygiene, or cleanness, in modern developed countries may be making people sick in unexpected ways.

This idea is called the Hygiene Hypothesis (a hypothesis is a possible explanation that has not yet been proved). It may explain the rising rates of autoimmune diseases—sicknesses in which the body's natural immune system fails to work properly, or attacks things it shouldn't, like the cells of its own body.

Asthma, allergies, multiple sclerosis, and inflammatory bowel disease are just some of the autoimmune diseases that are becoming more common in the industrialized world. One reason may be that children in developed countries are exposed to fewer childhood infections than they used to be. In addition, fewer children today grow up on farms, which have a variety of animals, crops, and microogranisms. These conditions and environments challenge the immune system, which, like a muscle, needs exercise in order to develop properly. Colds, animal hair, dirt, and minor infections are threats that force kids' immune systems into action. Without such challenges, the immune systems may not know how to function properly later in life—and if immune systems fail to act when they should, or go into overdrive when they are not needed, people get seriously sick.

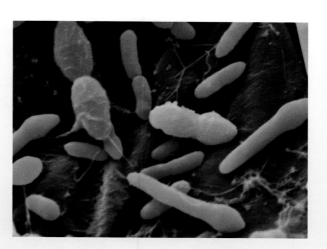

Artificial color has been used in this electron microscope photograph to highlight the different types bacteria commonly found in human feces. Although doctors agree that hand-washing and good sanitation are vital for preventing the spread of disease, some fear that our quest for super-cleanliness may be undermining our health.

If the Hygiene Hypothesis is true, should we all start rolling around in the dirt? Not necessarily. But the medical profession could respond by treating early childhood infections in ways that allow the immune system to develop properly, or by creating products and practices that challenge young people's immune systems in safe ways. Much research remains to be done on the Hygiene Hypothesis, but medical researchers are seeking an answer to the question: Have we become too clean for our own good?

These *Straphylococcus aureus* bacteria are multiplying rapidly through cell division. A drug-resistant form of this bacterium is responsible for the contagious disease known as MRSA.

between medicine and bacteria, researchers are working on new antibiotics to combat MRSA and other drug-resistant "super-bugs."

The deadly properties of bacteria have been harnessed as weapons. In 1984, religious cultists contaminated a salad bar in Oregon with *Salmonella* bacteria, causing an outbreak of food poisoning. No one died in that attack, but in 2001 letters contaminated with anthrax infected twenty-two Americans, five of whom died. Although the source of the anthrax attacks remains unknown, the tragedies alerted governments, public health workers, and citizens to the potential dangers of bioterrorism—attacks using biological agents such as bacteria.

THE BENEFITS OF BACTERIA

Bacteria create a lot of trouble for people, but they also give big benefits. Beyond helping us digest our food, they help make some of it. Bacteria, especially members of the genus *Lactobacillus,* are necessary to many food-making processes, such as fermenting, curdling, and pickling. Soy sauce, cheese, yogurt, pickles, and wine are just a few of the foods that would not exist without bacteria.

Bacteria are a key part of the growing business of designing genetically engineered foods and crops. Among the bacterially modified products already in the marketplace are potatoes and corn with a gene from *Bacillus thuringiensis* added to their genome to protect them from destructive beetles. Genetically modified soybean plants now carry a bacterial gene that prevents them from being killed by agricultural weed-killers. Although some people worry that genetically modified foods may cause unsuspected health or environmental problems, the U.S. government and others around the world have approved such products, and the march to develop new ones is under way. Researchers are examining hundreds of species

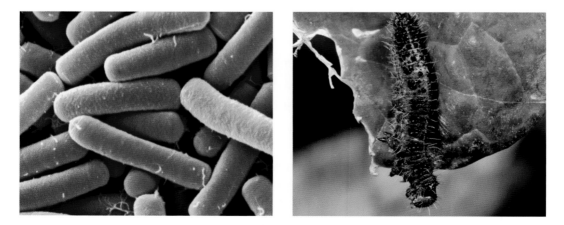

Bacillus thuringensis (left) produces proteins that are poisonous to plant pests such as gypsy moths and tent caterpillars. A leaf-eating caterpillar that has been treated with *B. thuringensis* (right) has died—a success story for bacterial pest control.

Pseudomonas putida bacteria (left) have been proven to break down petroleum products into less environmentally harmful substances. Droplets of oil (right) were consumed by bacterial colonies, which appear as faint blotches, in six hours.

of bacteria to see what useful or valuable traits their genes can lend to other organisms.

Bacteria have industrial and environmental uses, too. Fertilizer has long been used as an aid to cleaning up oil spills, because it encourages the growth of bacteria that eat the carbon compounds in petroleum. Naturally occurring bacteria can be an effective tool for removing other toxins and wastes from the environment, too. The metabolic activity of the bacteria either consumes unwanted substances such as plastics, medicines, and metals or changes them into less harmful ones. Although this approach to solving environmental problems is in its early stages, it holds great promise.

In addition to using natural bacteria, scientists are genetically altering bacteria to make them even more useful. *Deinococcus radiodurans,* for example, is highly resistant to radiation, able to survive and grow in radioactive environments that would kill other microbes. Genetic engineers are working to tailor this bacterium for use in treating one of the most dangerous environmental hazards: radioactive waste. As with all genetic engineering

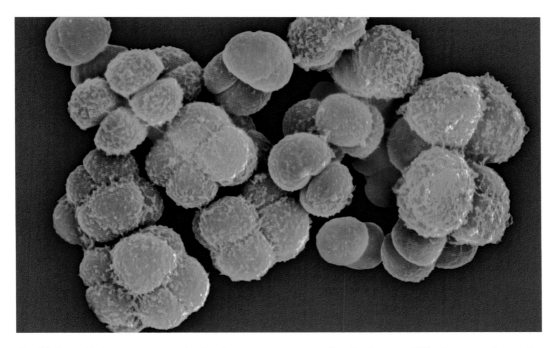

Could these *Deinococcus* bacteria be the answer to one of today's most difficult waste-disposal problems? The bacteria have a high tolerance for radiation and may be engineered to consume radioactive waste from nuclear power plants.

projects, however, there are concerns that releasing a genetically altered microbe into the environment may have unexpected effects.

Two of the biggest benefits of bacteria are all around us. They are soil and air. Bacteria are major contributors, along with fungi and other microorganisms, to the endless, planet-wide process of recycling that breaks down dead plants and animals, turning them into fertile soil and nutrients that other life forms can use. And photosynthetic bacteria, metabolizing away for millions of years, turned Earth's early carbon-dioxide-heavy atmosphere into an atmosphere that could support oxygen-breathing life forms—including, eventually, human beings. Bacteria are and always have been a vital part of the earth's ecosystems. They have made this planet into a living world.

ARCHAEA

DOMAIN Archaea

KINGDOM Monerans

PHYLUM Crenarchaeotes
Euryarchaeotes
*Korarchaeotes

* not yet verified

FAMILY TREES

BACTERIA

Bacteria

Monerans

Acidobacteria
Actinobacteria
Aquificae
Bacteroidetes
Chlamydiae
Chlorobi
Chloroflexi
Chrysiogenetes
Cyanobacteria
Deferribacteres
Deinococcus-Thermus
Dictyoglomi
Fibrobacteres
Firmicutes
Fusobacteria
Gemmatomonadetes
Lentisphaerae
Nitrospira
Planctomycetes
Proteobacteria
Spirochaetes
Verrucomicrobia
Thermodesulfobacteria
Thermomicrobia
Thermotogae

B I B L I O G R A P H Y

The author found these resources especially helpful when researching this book.

Boyd, Robert S. "They're little killers, and they're on our side," *Oregonian*, January 16, 2008, online at http://www.oregonlive.com/metro/oregonian/index.ssf?/base/science/1200376507214770.xml&coll=7

Garrity, George M., Timothy G. Lilburn, James R. Cole, Scott H. Harrison, Jean Euzeby, Brian J. Tindall, *The Taxonomic Outline of Bacteria and Archaea*, TOBA Release 7.7, online at http://www.taxonomicoutline.org/index.php/toba/index

Lecointre, Guillaume and Hervé Le Guyader. *The Tree of Life: A Phylogenetic Classification*. Translated by Dominique Visset. Cambridge, MA: Belknap Press, 2006.

Sachs, Jessica Snyder. *Good Germs, Bad Germs: Health and Survival in a Bacterial World*. New York: Hill and Wang, 2007.

Singleton, Paul. *Bacteria in Biology, Biotechnology, and Medicine*. 6th edition. Chicester, UK: John Wiley & Sons, 2004.

Tudge, Colin. *The Variety of Life*. New York: Oxford University Press, 2000.

University of Michigan Health System (2007, September 9). "The Hygiene Hypothesis: Are Cleanlier Lifestyles Causing More Allergies For Kids?" Online at http://www.sciencedaily.com/releases/2007/09/070905174501.htm

Wassenaar, Trudy M. "Bacteria: More Than Pathogens." ActionBioscience.org, July 2002. Online at http://www.actionbioscience.org/biodiversity/wassenaar.html

I N D E X

Page numbers in **boldface** are illustrations.

A B O U T   T H E   A U T H O R

Rebecca Stefoff is the author of many books on scientific subjects for young readers. She has explored the world of plants and animals in Marshall Cavendish's Living Things series and in several volumes of the AnimalWays series, also published by Marshall Cavendish. For the Family Trees series, she has written books on primates, flowering plants, marsupials, fungi, and more. Stefoff has also written about evolution in *Charles Darwin and the Evolution Revolution* (Oxford University Press, 1996), and she appeared in the *A&E Biography* program on Darwin and his work. Stefoff lives in Portland, Oregon. You can learn more about her books for young readers at www.rebeccastefoff.com.